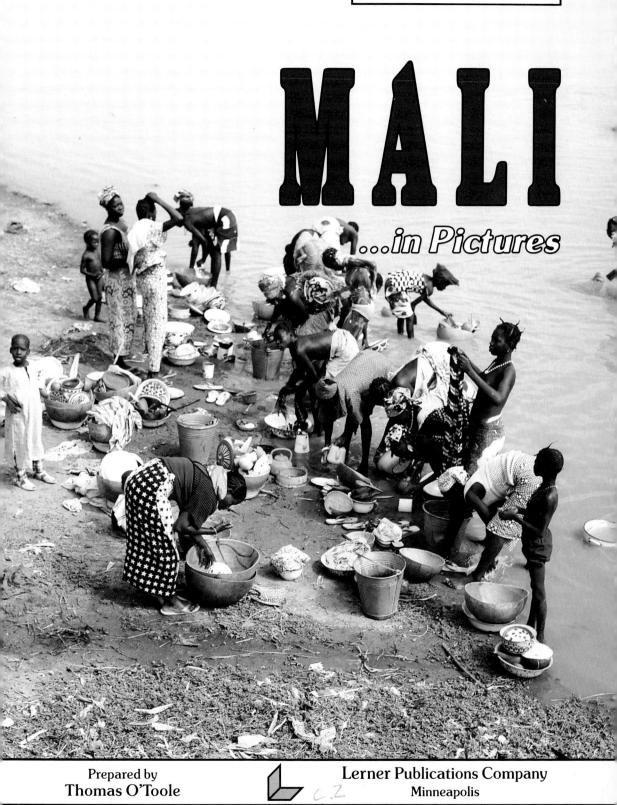

MALI

...in Pictures

Prepared by
Thomas O'Toole

Lerner Publications Company
Minneapolis

Courtesy of Deborah Dyson

Three young Malians display one of their handmade toys.

This book is a newly commissioned title in the Visual Geography Series. The text is set in 10/12 Century Textbook.

LIBRARY OF CONGRESS CATALOGING-IN-PUBLICATION DATA

O'Toole, Thomas, 1941-

Mali in pictures / prepared by Thomas O'Toole.
  p. cm. — (Visual geography series)
  Includes index.
  Summary: Text and photographs introduce the topography, history, society, economy, and governmental structure of Mali.
  ISBN 0-8225-1869-4 (lib. bdg.)
  1. Mali. [1. Mali.] I. Title.   II. Series.   III. Series: Visual geography series (Minneapolis, Minn.)
DT551.22.086   1990   89-34527
966.23—dc20   CIP
                                            AC

International Standard Book Number: 0-8225-1869-4
Library of Congress Card Catalog Number: 89-34527

VISUAL GEOGRAPHY SERIES®

Publisher
Harry Jonas Lerner
Associate Publisher
Nancy M. Campbell
Senior Editor
Mary M. Rodgers
Editors
Gretchen Bratvold
Dan Filbin
Photo Researcher
Karen A. Sirvaitis
Editorial/Photo Assistant
Marybeth Campbell
Consultants/Contributors
Thomas O'Toole
Sandra K. Davis
Designer
Jim Simondet
Cartographer
Carol F. Barrett
Indexers
Kristine S. Schubert
Sylvia Timian
Production Manager
Gary J. Hansen

Independent Picture Service

A member of Mali's Soninke people wears traditional jewelry and a headdress.

Acknowledgments

Title page courtesy of Deborah Dyson.

Elevation contours adapted from *The Times Atlas of the World,* seventh comprehensive edition (New York: Times Books, 1985).

1 2 3 4 5 6 7 8 9 10 99 98 97 96 95 94 93 92 91 90

A local market in Mopti—a city in central Mali near the Niger River—offers wide-mouthed jars for sale.

Contents

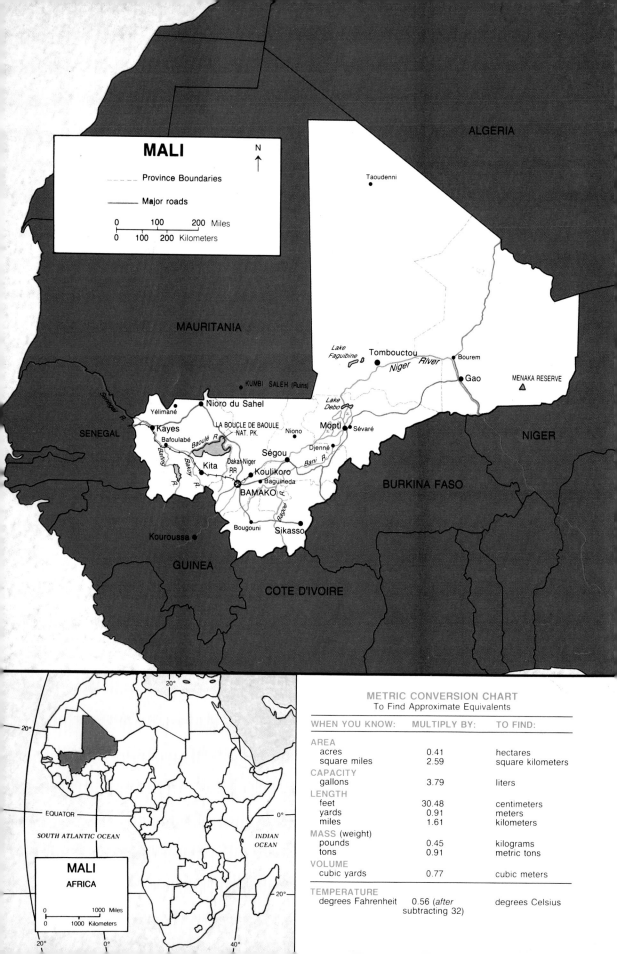

MALI

N ↑

Province Boundaries
Major roads

0   100   200 Miles
0 100 200 Kilometers

ALGERIA

Taoudenni

MAURITANIA

KUMBI SALEH (Ruins)

Lake
Faguibine
Tombouctou
Niger   River   Bourem
Gao
MENAKA RESERVE

Nioro du Sahel

Yélimané
Lake
Debo
SENEGAL
Kayes   LA BOUCLE DE BAOULE   Mopti
Bafoulabé   NAT. PK.   Niono   Sévaré
Baoulé R.
Djenné
Ségou
Kita   Bani R.
Dakar-Niger
RR   Koulikoro
Baguineda
BAMAKO
NIGER

BURKINA FASO

Bougouni   Sikasso

Kouroussa

GUINEA

COTE D'IVOIRE

20°

20°
20°

EQUATOR   0°

SOUTH ATLANTIC OCEAN   INDIAN
OCEAN

MALI
AFRICA

0   1000 Miles
0   1000 Kilometers

20°
0°   40°

METRIC CONVERSION CHART
To Find Approximate Equivalents

WHEN YOU KNOW:	MULTIPLY BY:	TO FIND:
AREA		
acres	0.41	hectares
square miles	2.59	square kilometers
CAPACITY		
gallons	3.79	liters
LENGTH		
feet	30.48	centimeters
yards	0.91	meters
miles	1.61	kilometers
MASS (weight)		
pounds	0.45	kilograms
tons	0.91	metric tons
VOLUME		
cubic yards	0.77	cubic meters
TEMPERATURE		
degrees Fahrenheit	0.56 (*after* subtracting 32)	degrees Celsius

The mud houses of Mali's Dogon people occupy some of the country's rockiest land. Yet the group's hardworking farmers are able to raise a variety of crops.

Introduction

A landlocked country in West Africa, Mali lies in the western Sudan—a broad region of the African continent just south of the Sahara Desert. The nation was once the home of the great empires of Ghana, Mali, and Songhai. For centuries, these rich empires traded gold and slaves for salt and textiles from markets along the Mediterranean Sea. In modern times, however, Mali ranks among the world's poorest countries.

Islamic armies from North Africa conquered Mali in the eleventh century, and most of the area's people gradually accepted the Islamic religion. Between the sixteenth and the nineteenth centuries, slave raiders supplied people to the European slave trade.

By the 1800s, some Africans wanted to spread Islam throughout West Africa. They also hoped to prevent Europeans—particularly the French—from taking over remote areas of the Sudan. With these goals in mind, African leaders established several small states, which included much of Mali's land. By the late 1890s, French troops had subdued the forces of the Islamic realms, and France made the territory part of its African colonial empire.

Along with other French territories in West Africa, Mali achieved independence in 1960. Since then, only two presidents have governed the nation. Modibo Keita ran a single-party state from 1960 to 1968. In that year, Moussa Traoré led a government takeover, and since 1969 he has been Mali's chief executive.

In recent years, Mali has suffered severe droughts that have turned large portions of the country into desert. Unpredictable rainfall has affected traditional living patterns and livelihoods. Many of the nation's

Courtesy of United Nations

Daily activity stops in front of Mopti's main mosque (Islamic place of worship) when the muezzin, or crier, calls faithful Muslims (followers of Islam) to prayer.

6

Some of the herders of northern Mali belong to the Tuareg ethnic group. They protect their heads from the dry heat and blowing sands of the Sahara Desert with cloth veils.

herders—such as the Fulbé and the Tuareg, who live in central and northern Mali—lost much of their livestock as water and pasture became scarce. In addition, many Malians died, and others suffered from malnutrition as a result of frequently poor harvests. Mali's exports of cotton and peanuts—its main source of foreign income—dropped.

The Traoré regime is attempting to address some of these problems. But mismanagement and government corruption hamper national efforts. Recent plans to put public finances in order and to reorganize the farming sector have attracted foreign aid. Yet the challenges of too few resources, decreasing export income, and chronic food shortages remain.

A young farmer in northwestern Mali milks his goat. The region suffered severe shortages of rainfall in the 1980s, and many people and livestock died of starvation.

Only sturdy, sure-footed animals, such as donkeys and camels, are able to cross the sandy hillsides of northern Mali.

1) The Land

Mali—a large, landlocked country on the western side of the African continent—covers an area of about 465,000 square miles. The nation is almost three times the size of the state of California. Algeria borders Mali to the north, and Niger is Mali's eastern neighbor. To the south lie Guinea, Côte d'Ivoire, and Burkina Faso. Mauritania and Senegal share Mali's western boundary.

Topography

Mali's generally flat territory consists of three principal regions. The Sahara Desert cuts into northern Mali. In the center of the country lies the Sahel, a semi-arid transition zone between the northern desert and southern grasslands. Fertile savanna (grassland) covers southern Mali, where farmers grow crops.

Northern Mali is part of the Sahara Desert, a vast barren land that also extends into other countries in northern Africa. Most of the desert is made up of rocky plains dotted with occasional thorny shrubs. In some places, a region of shifting sands, called an *erg*, appears. The largest ergs in Mali are Sekkane Erg, which lies in the center of the country, and Chech Erg, which extends into Algeria. The Malian section of the Sahara also includes Adrar des Iforas, a mountainous region in the northeastern part of the country.

The Sahel, which means "shore" in Arabic, forms the southern edge of the Sahara. About 20 percent of Africa's land—over 11 million square miles—is included in the Sahel. In Mali, the region covers a narrow belt of semi-arid territory where herders raise livestock despite drought conditions. The animals eat the scrubby vegetation, and the herders lead the livestock to seasonal watering holes.

Below the Sahel is a vast inland delta, or fertile floodland, formed by the Niger and Bani rivers. This 40,000-square-mile area contains some of the richest agricultural land in Africa. Two of the region's bodies of water—Lake Debo and Lake Faguibine—retain water even in the dry season.

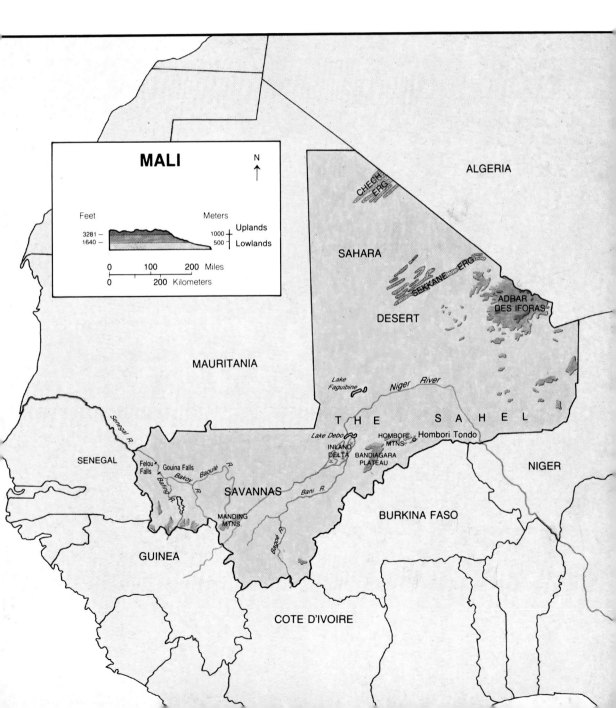

Pitted cliffs of the Bandiagara Plateau have been home to the Dogon for centuries. The rocky plateau stretches diagonally from southwestern to northeastern Mali.

Rivers

Two large rivers—the Senegal and the Niger—provide Mali with water. Rising in Guinea and flowing northeast for 560 miles, the Senegal River is broken in Mali first by the Gouina Falls and then, near Kayes, by the Felou Falls. Eventually, the river cuts through Senegal and Mauritania before emptying into the Atlantic Ocean. Rainfall causes the Senegal's water level to rise in July and to stay high until October. In April, however, at the end of the dry season, the river is often reduced to a shallow stream. The Senegal's tributaries—including the Bakoy, the Bafing, and the

Although most of the southern part of the country is level, several elevated features appear. The Bandiagara Plateau is a series of cliffs that runs for about 150 miles from southwest to northeast. Some of these cliffs are 1,200 feet high. The Hombori Mountains are made of sandstone, and a few of the range's flat-topped peaks exceed 3,000 feet. One of these heights, named Hombori Tondo, rises to 3,789 feet and is Mali's tallest point. From the nation's western border to about 50 miles east of the capital city of Bamako are the Manding Mountains. These highlands climb to 1,500 feet above sea level.

West of the city of Sikasso in southern Mali, outflow from the Bagoé River tumbles over a cliff.

The Niger, Africa's third longest river, fills with water in the rainy season and floods over its banks.

Baoulé—irrigate the land between the southwestern towns of Kayes and Kita.

The Niger River flows through much of the rest of Mali. The third longest waterway in Africa, the Niger begins its 2,600-mile course in Guinea and travels northeast for more than 600 miles. In east central Mali, the Niger arches in a southeastern direction, forming a curve called the Niger Bend. The river then continues to the Gulf of Guinea, which is an arm of the Atlantic Ocean.

Following the course of a river, women carry produce to sell in the town of Bandiagara.

Both the Niger and the Senegal rivers are major transportation routes during Mali's rainy season. Between Kouroussa in Guinea and Gao in eastern Mali, the Niger accommodates a variety of boats for at least three months every year. The Bani, the Niger's main tributary in Mali, is also an important sea-lane for both goods and people.

Climate

Since the nation's temperatures are fairly hot year-round, Malians use the country's annual cycle of rainfall to mark the seasons. In addition, winds affect the rainfall and temperature levels. Hot, dry gusts called *harmattans* kick up dust and bring high temperatures to the north. Winds from the Gulf of Guinea carry moisture and slightly lower temperatures to southern Mali.

The Sahara Desert, where rain rarely falls, often experiences temperatures of 120° F and has highs of 140° F. In the Sahel, rainfall varies from 7 to 20 inches a year, and temperatures generally stay between 80° and 100° F. Although drought is a normal feature of the Sahel, more serious shortages of rain have occurred in the last two decades.

Just south of the Sahel, rainfall averages about 20 inches per year. In the far south of Mali, rainy seasons of varying lengths begin in May or June and end in late October. This region receives about 60 inches

Boatmen skillfully use poles to push their vessel through the waters of the Niger River. During the wet season, the waterway ferries people and their goods to many parts of Mali.

of rainfall annually. Temperatures range between 75° and 95° F throughout southern Mali.

Flora and Fauna

In general, Mali has three areas of vegetation. Only thorny shrubs can survive the harsh conditions of the Sahara Desert. Droughts in the 1970s and 1980s have extended the desert southward, perhaps permanently, and few plant species remain.

The Sahel zone is sparsely vegetated, mostly with trees that can withstand long periods without rain. Along the Sahel's northern edge and in other isolated areas, small, thorny acacia trees and cram-cram grass grow. In the southern areas of the Sahel, the doom palm and the baobab tree, which holds water in its barkless trunk, stand out on the landscape.

Mali's wooded grasslands begin south of Bamako, and some forests are located along the region's rivers. Shea trees and silk-cotton trees are most common, and Malians plant many mango fruit trees in

Courtesy of Lester and Rosemary Moeller

The setting sun helps to define the shape of a baobab tree. The thick tissue of the plant's trunk stores water, allowing the tree to survive in hot, dry climates.

A family of herders in the Sahel—a semidesert area in northern Mali—lets their livestock feed on the region's scrub vegetation.

Photo by The Hutchison Library

Courtesy of Mark La Pointe

Grasping leaves with its strong lips, a hungry camel reaches for its midday meal. The lining of the animal's mouth is extremely tough, permitting camels to eat even thorny cactus plants.

the area. This region also contains Mali's farmland, where small plots yield cereal grains, root crops, and cotton.

For centuries, Malian farmers have cleared the land to grow food. Because this activity destroys animal habitats, little wildlife remains in the country. Researchers have reported a limited number of lions at the Niger Bend, on the Bandiagara Plateau, and in western Mali. Elephants now live only near the Niger Bend and around the Bani River, and giraffes roam the west bank of the Niger near Gao and Bourem. Several different kinds of antelope make their homes in scattered areas of the country. Hippopotamuses inhabit the Niger and the Bani, eating the vegetation that grows in and around the rivers. Many species of birds, including an occasional

ostrich, thrive in the inland delta and the Niger Bend.

Some licensed hunting and considerable poaching (illegal killing) occur in the two national game reserves—La Boucle de Baoulé National Park in the west and Ménaka Reserve in the east. Giraffes, elephants, antelope, lions, and hippos inhabit these semi-protected areas.

Cities and Towns

Mali is an overwhelmingly rural country, and its cities are small. More than 80 percent of the nation's 8.9 million people practice subsistence agriculture—a style of farming that feeds only a single family. Throughout the country are many villages with fewer than 1,000 people. Most of these

14

settlements lie in the valleys of the Niger, Senegal, and Bani rivers or in areas where rainfall is plentiful.

BAMAKO

Bamako, Mali's capital and largest city, has about 800,000 people. The majority of them, however, earn at least part of their living from rural activities, such as herding, fishing, and crop farming. When Mali gained independence in 1960, Bamako was a quiet, shady place on the western bank of the Niger River. As job opportunities became available in the capital, the population grew rapidly. The city expanded to the eastern bank, absorbing the small villages that were located there.

The commercial and administrative center of the nation, Bamako has a lively and crowded market area. The city also contains a handful of stores and other service establishments and the Grand Mosque (an Islamic place of prayer). Lavish residences, important governmental offices, and religious buildings complete the main area of the capital.

The rest of Bamako—which stretches outward into more than 20 neighborhoods, called *quartiers* (quarters)—has evolved in a less-planned fashion. Modern houses with running water and electricity are scattered throughout the city. Constructed of cement, these homes belong to wealthy government officials and middle-income foreigners. Most Malians in Bamako live in dwellings built of mud bricks. Some neighborhoods consist of run-down shacks, where people struggle to survive because they have no jobs.

SECONDARY URBAN CENTERS

Besides Bamako, few other places in Mali have large populations. Most of the big towns developed around former colonial stations. Some of these urban centers are expanding because of the growth of local industries.

Just outside the capital city of Bamako, clean laundry is laid out to dry. Located along the Niger River, the city supports about 800,000 inhabitants.

Courtesy of Deborah Dyson

An aerial view of Bamako shows clusters of flat-roofed houses stretching outward from the center. The twin towers of the Grand Mosque *(top right)* are prominent on the cityscape.

Stalls in the capital's large market offer a variety of goods, including food, beads, blankets, gold, and African spices.

Vendors in a section of the market at Mopti sell handwoven mats. The sign indicates that the area is also a major fishing port, whose facilities have been financed by a European development fund.

Located along the Niger River, Ségou (population 75,000) is Mali's second largest population center. Once the capital of a nineteenth-century African realm, the city also contains many colonial-era buildings from its days as a French outpost. The Bambara—one of Mali's major ethnic groups—are the main vendors in Ségou's market, offering masks, pottery, and food for sale.

Situated on several islets where the Bani and the Niger rivers join, Mopti (population 60,000) is an important Islamic center and marketplace, chiefly for the nation's fish industry. The city is home to a mixture of Mali's many ethnic groups, including members of the Malinke, the Fulbé, the Songhai, and the Tukulors.

Sikasso (population 50,000) lies in the far southeastern part of the country, near Mali's border with Côte d'Ivoire. Located in a well-watered area, the city contains much of Mali's Senufo population. Historically, the Senufo resisted being absorbed by other powers—both European and African—and their distinct culture survives in villages surrounding Sikasso.

Kayes (population 48,000) lies in southwestern Mali along the Senegal River near the Senegal border. The Dakar-Niger Railway connects Dakar, the capital of Senegal, to Kayes. The line continues to Bamako

17

Photo by Piotr Kostrzewski

The streets of Tombouctou (also spelled Timbuktu), where merchants display rows of ripe fruits and vegetables, are covered with sand that has blown in from the Sahel.

developed civilizations. Some of these findings exist in the ruins of former cities, major trade stations, and Islamic centers. Other towns—such as Tombouctou (also spelled Timbuktu) Gao, and Djenné—still survive and have long histories.

Founded in about 1100, Tombouctou (population 20,000) is located eight miles from the Niger River in central Mali. A well-established trade hub, the city flourished between 1200 and 1591. Between the fourteenth and sixteenth centuries, Tombouctou was a place of Islamic learning and culture.

After Moroccan raiders from the northwest sacked Tombouctou in 1591, the city declined in importance and population. Shifting sands weakened the foundations of earthen buildings, most of which have since crumbled or are now half-buried. Several mosques remain standing, however. In modern times, little trade occurs, except the yearly camel caravan that brings salt from northern mines.

Located on the Niger River in central Mali, Gao (population 33,000) was once the capital of the Songhai Empire. This domain flourished in the fifteenth and sixteenth centuries. Although, like Tombouctou, Gao declined at the end of the imperial era, this city has made a comeback. Planners rebuilt much of Gao in the twentieth century, and it is now a small, thriving river port. Wide, unpaved streets crisscross Gao. Most buildings, however, are poorly constructed and often are crowded with people.

Archaeologists believe that Djenné, located in south central Mali, is one of the oldest settlements in West Africa. Founded in the ninth century, Djenné reached its height as a marketplace and Islamic center between the fourteenth and sixteenth centuries. In modern times, the town has only 8,000 residents. Djenné's famous mud mosque, however, draws visitors to the region. An excellent example of the local architectural style, the building requires yearly repairs after annual rains soften its exterior.

and Koulikoro, Mali. Kayes also has a vital role as a port city. In the rainy season, boats can travel west from Kayes to Saint-Louis—a Senegalese port along the Atlantic Ocean.

Historic Sites

As the center of several important African realms, Mali contains evidence of highly

Djenné attracts visitors from throughout the world who come to see the town's mud mosque. Constructed in 1905, the house of prayer is structurally supported by thick columns, which help to prevent the building from collapsing in the rainy season.

Photo by Ullstein

A long line of camels crosses the Sahara Desert. Camel caravans became the means by which Mali kept up trade contacts with regions to the north. The income from these caravans funded and strengthened the area's early empires.

2) History and Government

Cave paintings found in the Sudan reveal part of Mali's early history. This artistic evidence and other archaeological clues tell the story not only of the Malian people but of groups in nearby countries, such as Senegal, Mauritania, Guinea, and Niger.

Roughly 10,000 years ago, the southern Sahara had a wet climate. Heavy rainfall created huge, shallow lakes and rivers in the region. Cave paintings depict large animals—such as giraffes, elephants, hippopotamuses, and rhinoceroses—that inhabited the Sahara's well-irrigated grasslands and forests. Water animals—crocodiles and fish, for example—also appear in the cave illustrations.

The lakes and rivers were abundant sources of fish and attracted Stone-Age peoples who lived in the region. Families of fishermen and hunters began to live near these life-supporting bodies of water. In time, semi-permanent and permanent settlements formed.

About 4000 B.C., however, the rainfall that had enriched the southern Sahara began to decrease, and the region became drier and hotter. As the lakes evaporated, the local people learned to gather root crops and to raise livestock. Eventually, the dry weather reduced food supplies and forced many populations south, away from the expanding desert into the inland delta of the Niger.

Villages developed on the west central borders of present-day Mali. The new residents cleared the forest to plant grain and used the grasslands to feed their livestock. Climate changes, as well as the removal of most of the local vegetation, helped the desert to spread even farther. By the fifth century B.C., the Sahara was well established.

The desert might have cut off contact between the Mediterranean coast and the south if not for the introduction of camels. Middle Eastern traders brought these hump-backed animals to the Sahara in about A.D. 100. Because they could withstand long periods without water, camels became the main form of desert transportation.

The Great Empires

By about A.D. 300, enough people lived in some parts of Mali to support trading centers and kingdoms. Most of these political units were made up of small villages, where local leaders exercised informal control.

From these loosely organized kingdoms emerged a series of three strong and prosperous trading empires. Each had its economic foundation in the control of Saharan commercial routes, which led to Mediterranean and Asian markets. Camel caravans crossed the Sahara, carrying cloth, salt, and other products to regions south of the desert. The traders returned to northern Africa with gold, leather goods, and slaves.

THE GHANA EMPIRE

A federation of kingdoms called the Ghana Empire evolved about A.D. 300. It developed from the farming settlements that existed in what are now southwestern Mali and southeastern Mauritania. The empire had its capital at Kumbi Saleh (in Mauritania near the border with Mali) and reached its height between A.D. 700 and A.D. 1075.

Members of the Soninke people established the empire as a great trading center and made nearby ethnic groups subjects of their realm. Commercial caravans journeyed from the capital—as well as from towns such as Audagost and Walata—through the desert to the Mediterranean coast. The empire controlled major parts

Mined in northern Mali, slabs of salt were a major trade item of the Ghana Empire. Workers broke the blocks into granules, which could be used to flavor and preserve food. Southern traders exchanged gold and slaves for the salt from the north.

Photo by Piotr Kostrzewski

of these routes, which were the only known paths through the Sahara. Ghana also developed roads that went south to the Gulf of Guinea.

Emperors charged taxes on goods that traveled along their commercial routes. The resulting income allowed the empire to keep a large army. This strong military organization ensured the realm's authority over vital trade links.

Many of the merchants with whom the Soninke traders came in contact were Arabs from areas north and east of the empire. By the seventh century A.D., these Arabs had accepted a new, one-god religion called Islam. Traders brought the faith to North Africa and within 100 years had passed it on to the Berbers. This local people controlled northern sections of the Saharan traffic.

In 1076 the Almoravids—an Islamic Berber dynasty (family of rulers)—sent troops to destroy the Ghana Empire and to take over its trade routes. Almoravid forces seized Kumbi Saleh, making the realm an Islamic state. Although Soninke warriors recaptured the city about 15 years later, the Ghana Empire continued to decline. During this period, people from Sosso—a kingdom ruled by Ghana—revolted, and by 1203 Sosso troops had gained control of the capital.

THE MALI EMPIRE

The Mali Empire developed in the 1200s from a small Malinke kingdom located near the present-day boundary between Mali and Guinea. The Malinke kingdom, which was under Ghana's and later under Sosso's authority, desired self-rule. A Malinke warrior-prince named Sundiata led a war of independence against the Sosso kingdom in about 1230. He combined many other small Malinke units into one realm to form the Mali Empire. It was centered in the capital city of Niani (now in Guinea).

At its height in the thirteenth and fourteenth centuries, the empire included parts of present-day Mali, Senegal, Gambia, Guinea, Mauritania, Burkina Faso, and Niger.

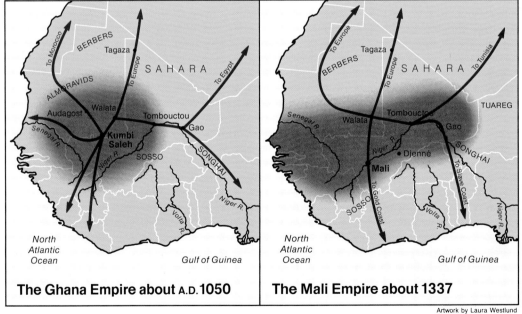

The Ghana Empire about A.D. 1050

The Mali Empire about 1337

Artwork by Laura Westlund

The successive Ghana and Mali empires flourished between A.D. 700 and A.D. 1400. The two realms overlapped in area, and each maintained overland routes to the Mediterranean Sea (in the north) and to the Gulf of Guinea (in the south).

In the mid-fourteenth century, the Malian *mansa* (emperor) Musa made Tombouctou into a major center for the study of the Islamic religion. A later visitor—the nineteenth-century French explorer René-Auguste Caillié—drew this image of the old city when he visited it in 1828. Caillié had strong impressions of Tombouctou. He praised its people as gentle and intelligent and described its buildings as clean and well designed.

Although the majority of Mali's subjects held traditional African beliefs, the ruler and government officials were Muslims (followers of Islam).

Under the Malinke *mansa* (emperor) Musa, who reigned between 1312 and about 1337, Mali became well known to the Islamic world. In 1324 the ruler made the hajj—a pilgrimage (religious visit) to the sacred Islamic city of Mecca in Saudi Arabia. The monarch traveled overland by way of the Sahara Desert—a long, hard journey that suggested the ruler's confidence in his guides. His willingness to be absent from the realm also emphasized his strong hold on the Mali throne.

The visit left strong impressions on Mansa Musa's subjects. Hundreds of people accompanied the emperor, who increased his importance by distributing large amounts of gold to people all along the route to Mecca. As a result of this lavish journey, trans-Saharan trade increased dramatically, and Islamic scholars came to Mali. Soon after Mansa Musa's return, the commercial city of Gao came under Mali's control. In addition, the emperor established Tombouctou as an important Islamic center.

Independent Picture Service

Camel-riding forces of the Tuareg took over Malian territory in the late fourteenth and early fifteenth centuries. In modern times, some members of the group continue to use camels as a major means of desert transportation.

The vast Mali Empire required the firm attention of skilled leaders, but few of Mansa Musa's successors had the qualities necessary to keep the realm together. Gradually, outlying areas came under the authority of other groups, including the Songhai and the Tuareg. By the fifteenth century, Songhai military successes had weakened the Mali Empire.

THE SONGHAI EMPIRE

Long established as a minor realm, the Songhai Empire increased in size and strength beginning in the mid-1300s. It soon began to absorb more territory, chiefly by taking over the Saharan trade routes that the Mali Empire once held.

The Songhai emperor Sonni Ali, who reigned from 1464 to 1492, stabilized the empire by making better laws and by expanding trade. Sonni Ali's forces conquered Tombouctou and Djenné, two important cultural and trading hubs in West Africa. The regime established its own capital at Gao in central Mali.

Sonni Ali's eventual successor, Askia Muhammad, brought the Songhai Empire to its peak in the early sixteenth century. Under his rule, the realm stretched from the Atlantic coast to Nigeria and included most of the former Mali Empire. The government efficiently administered the richest domain in West Africa. The emperor encouraged his subjects to adopt Islam, and he restored Tombouctou as an important Islamic center.

The sons of Askia Muhammad forced him to give up his throne in 1528, and the empire declined as his successors fought one another for control. Outsiders saw the realm's internal weakness as an opportunity to invade. The Songhai Empire survived several clashes until 1591, when the Moroccan leader Ahmed al-Mansur attacked with heavily armed soldiers. Lacking weaponry of equal force, the Songhai army was defeated near Gao in the Battle of Tondibi.

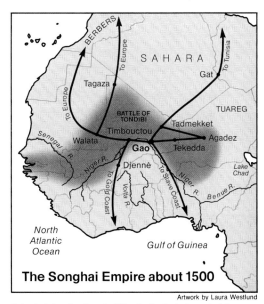
Artwork by Laura Westlund

At its height, the Songhai Empire included most of the area of present-day Mali. For about 200 years, Songhai's leaders controlled ancient trade routes and shaped the realm into a strong Islamic state.

The Moroccans used places like Tombouctou as outposts for the trade in gold and slaves that they conducted with ports on the Mediterranean Sea. In general, however, the Moroccans weakly governed the region.

New Kingdoms, the Slave Trade, and the Spread of Islam

After the decline of the great empires, a number of small realms developed in central Mali. Among these domains were the Fulbé kingdom of Macina (1400–1862), the Bambara kingdom of Ségou (1600–1862), and the Bambara kingdom of Kaarta (1633–1854). Initially, the wealth of these kingdoms was based on raising livestock and on farming the land. Later—partly in response to European demands for slaves—the realms prospered by capturing and sending people to trading stations on the Atlantic coast. To some extent, the kingdoms of Kaarta and Ségou were founded on the profits of slavery.

Throughout Africa, slavery had been an ongoing economic activity for many centuries. Beginning in the late sixteenth century, however, Europeans began to buy and trade more slaves. The traders were responding to calls for cheap labor from plantation owners in newly acquired European colonies. European buyers and the leaders of some African states saw the increased demand for slaves as an opportunity to make money. Raiders captured thousands of people in Mali, transporting them to the coasts of present-day Senegal, Gambia, and Guinea.

Not all the slaves from Mali ended up on colonial estates. Some captives were sent to African states in the interior, and others

Independent Picture Service

For centuries, raiders had captured Africans to sell in local slave markets. Beginning in the late 1500s, European demands for slaves increased, and in time raiders traveled far into the African interior. The captives from Mali usually were forced to walk to trade stations on the Gulf of Guinea.

were sold to Middle Eastern markets. Those destined for European plantations traveled with large numbers of other Africans who became the living cargo of the slave trade. By the eighteenth century, slave raids had driven Dogon, Bambara, and Senufo peoples from their villages.

At about the same time, the ancient caravan routes across the Sahara shifted eastward because of internal warfare and dwindling supplies of precious goods in the west. As a result of this change, West Africa's waterways became major passageways for goods traded throughout the region. The shift to water routes benefited the Dyula, a people who managed much of the river traffic in West Africa.

Most Dyula were Muslims, and their constant movement in search of trade brought the Islamic religion to a wide audience. Another spur to the spread of Islam was the Fulbé kingdom, which supported *jihads*—holy wars to convert non-Muslims to the religion.

The 1800s

Amid these internal changes, European colonial powers began to affect Mali's boundaries. Coastal trade between Africa

Courtesy of Mark La Pointe

A sign in French identifies the house in Tombouctou where Caillié stayed in April and May of 1828. He was among the first Europeans to visit Mali.

and Europe had occurred for centuries, but explorations to the interior were rare until the early nineteenth century. Among the first Europeans to reach Malian territory was the Frenchman René-Auguste Caillié, who left North Africa in 1827. Disguising himself as an Arab, he traveled across the Sahara to Tombouctou.

Other European adventurers tried to map the course of the Niger River, and some—notably the Scottish doctor Mungo Park—died in the attempt. In 1830 the British explorer Richard Lander and his brother John traced the waterway to the Gulf of Guinea. As Europeans charted more of the West African interior, they became interested in bringing remote areas under colonial rule. Yet many parts of West Africa—particularly in Mali—had rarely been exposed to European authority, and strong African states governed these regions.

In the mid-nineteenth century, a local Tukulor family, the Tall dynasty, subdued the various Malian kingdoms that emerged after the fall of the Songhai Empire. Al-Hajj Umar, an Islamic scholar and skilled military commander, founded the Tukulor realm as the result of a jihad that he had launched in 1852. Preaching against what he thought were the corrupt practices of West African Muslims, Umar gathered a large following. In 1854 his troops conquered the Bambara kingdom of Kaarta (near present-day Nioro du Sahel, Mali), and they took Ségou and Macina in 1862. After Umar's death in 1864, his son, Ahmadu Tall, succeeded him in Ségou. Ahmadu's brother Mohammad Muntaga Tall ruled Kaarta, and their cousin Tijani Tall reigned over Macina.

In the late nineteenth century, Samory Touré, a strong Malinke leader, established political control over much of southern Mali. With his capital at Bissandougou, Samory attempted to reunite the former Mali Empire. His realm included the Bouré gold fields and the headwaters of the Niger River (both now in Guinea).

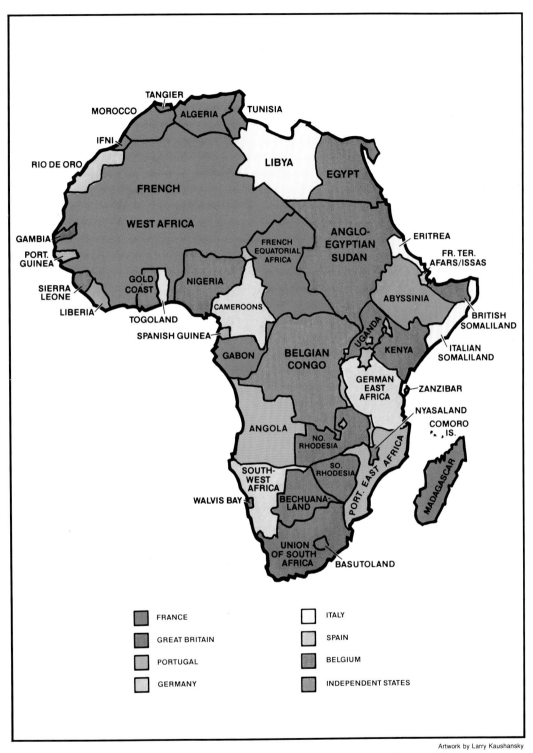

FRANCE	ITALY
GREAT BRITAIN	SPAIN
PORTUGAL	BELGIUM
GERMANY	INDEPENDENT STATES

By the late nineteenth century, European governments had divided Africa into areas of influence. Mali's territory became part of a large French federation called French West Africa. (Map information taken from *The Anchor Atlas of World History*, 1978.)

Jihads—holy wars to spread Islam—had brought the religion to most Malians by the end of the nineteenth century. The large number of mosques throughout the nation testify to the lasting impact of Islam on the population.

Ahmadu Tall, ruler of the Islamic Ségou kingdom, succeeded his father, Al-Hajj Umar, in 1864. French advances into Malian territory decreased Ahmadu's military and political strength. By 1892 the king had surrendered to French troops, signaling the beginning of Mali's colonial period.

The French constructed railway lines throughout French West Africa. Track connected Dakar, Senegal, to Kayes in southwestern Mali. Other branches went south to Abidjan in Côte d'Ivoire.

Courtesy of United Nations

French Colonization

Following their explorations of Africa, European powers established colonial spheres of influence on the continent. By the late 1800s, the European scramble for colonies was intense and endangered Mali's isolated position in the African interior.

France, which already had strong footholds in coastal areas of West Africa, decided to extend its claims inland in the 1880s. The French planned to build a trans-Saharan railroad, which would run through its colonial empire in Africa to the Mediterranean Sea. The French soon established forts at Kita and Bamako, and they completed a railway that reached from Dakar, Senegal, to Kayes and continued to the Niger River.

In order to fulfill their plans, the French began an all-out push for control of Mali. In 1887 they signed the Treaty of Bissandougou with Samory Touré. Under the agreement, the African ruler promised not to enlarge his domain north of the Niger River.

In 1889, however, Samory Touré rejected the treaty, and, for over a decade, he resisted France's efforts to expand its colonial holdings in West Africa. To secure his realm, Samory Touré also fought against other African kingdoms. Indeed, he often sold people into slavery to buy horses and weapons.

The Ségou kingdom of Ahmadu Tall surrendered to French troops in 1892, and the French captured Samory Touré in 1898. The fall from power of these two strong commanders signaled the end of African leadership in Mali for many decades. By 1900 the French flag flew over an enormous section of Africa, stretching from Senegal eastward to Lake Chad and northward to the Mediterranean Sea.

In 1904 France reorganized its territory in West Africa to form the Federation of French West Africa. It consisted of Senegal, French Guinea, Dahomey (now Benin),

By 1900 the three-part French flag — commonly called the tricolor — flew over colonial outposts in many parts of central and West Africa, including French Sudan (modern Mali).

Artwork by Laura Westlund

Côte d'Ivoire, and a large colony called Upper Senegal-Niger, which included most of present-day Mali. By 1920 regional unrest and the need to divide the large federation into smaller units caused France to redraw the federation's boundaries to form eight colonies. Senegal, French Guinea, Dahomey, and Côte d'Ivoire lost and gained territory. Upper Volta (modern Burkina Faso) absorbed some of Upper Senegal-Niger. Niger, Mauritania, and French Sudan (present-day Mali) composed the remainder of the new federation.

Colonial Rule

The governor of French Sudan ruled under the authority of the governor-general in Dakar—the headquarters of French West African administration. The governor-general, in turn, took his orders from the minister of colonies in France. This governmental framework had no place for African participation. In a few areas, such as Macina, Fulbé noble families maintained power by accepting French authority. They collected taxes and provided workers for French building projects.

By the 1930s, a small number of French-educated interpreters, teachers, office workers, and doctors' assistants staffed part of the colonial administration in French Sudan. This African group was never more than 5 percent of the colony's total population. The rest of the people became the object of a long-established French policy of "assimilation." The framers of this plan intended to give Africans a Western education and to absorb them into the greater French empire. The program was meant to break down traditional ethnic loyalties and to strengthen ties to France.

In a further effort to make French Sudan into a more valuable French colony, France imposed other colonial policies. The European nation obliged Africans to be an unpaid labor force on public-works projects. The French also drafted adult males for military service. Much of the interior remained under military control, and political activity was not permitted. Furthermore, the colonial legal system allowed suspected criminals to be imprisoned without trial. By the time World War II broke out in 1939, Africans in French Sudan were ready for change.

World War II to Independence

France fell to the forces of Nazi Germany in 1940, and the Germans set up a pro-Nazi government in Vichy, France. A resistance movement—called Free France—began operating in exile under General Charles de Gaulle. French officials in Africa were faced with a difficult decision. The choice was whether to be loyal to the Vichy government or to the forces of Free France. The governor of French Sudan declared his loyalty to the Vichy government. Many Africans in French Sudan, however, chose to support de Gaulle and Free France. Some fled to Liberia and to nearby British colonies to join the French war effort.

Hundreds of Africans from French Sudan served abroad in the armed forces of Free France. Within the colony, Africans grew rice and raised money to help the exiled French. In exchange for their participation, General de Gaulle promised the Africans in French Sudan a better life after the war. The experience of fighting for a

Courtesy of Library of Congress

During World War II (1939–1945), General Charles de Gaulle (above) **called on French citizens and colonists to join the war against Nazi Germany. Many Africans from French Sudan** (below) **responded by fighting alongside French and British troops in North Africa.**

Photo by UPI/Bettmann Newsphotos

Photo by UPI/Bettmann Newsphotos

Soon after World War II ended in 1945, Modibo Keita—a Malinke teacher—became part of the African Democratic Rally (RDA). This political party aimed to achieve independence from colonial rule by gathering the support of Africans throughout the continent.

Photo by UPI/Bettmann Newsphotos

Léopold Senghor of Senegal, another RDA member, became a close colleague of Keita's in the 1950s. After Mali and Senegal gained independence from France in 1958, the two former colonies united in 1959 to form the Mali Federation. The federation dissolved in 1960.

common goal unified Bambara, Senufo, and Dogon troops. When they returned home, many of the soldiers had come to see themselves as part of an African nation rather than as members of separate ethnic communities. This realization fueled a growing nationalist movement that sought self-rule for European colonies in Africa.

Western armies liberated France in 1944, and the war ended in 1945. Afterward, France revised its colonial policies regarding Africa and created a French Union. This group had a national assembly whose voting membership was evenly divided between France and its overseas colonies. The new union abolished forced labor and set up a federal council for all of French West Africa.

AFRICAN POLITICAL PARTIES

Many Africans were not convinced that France's view of the future was in their best interests. In 1946 West African leaders met in Bamako to found the continent's first interterritorial party—the Rassemblement Démocratique Africain (RDA, or African Democratic Rally). Locally, two of French Sudan's political organizations merged to form the Union Soudanaise-RDA. Under party leader Modibo Keita, the new organization expressed the colony's growing nationalism.

The French Union lasted until 1956, when African efforts resulted in some reforms, including more self-government for French Sudan. The colony's Africans were given equal voting rights with French citizens, and the territorial assembly was allowed to elect a council of ministers. The minister with the highest number of votes presided over this council as a prime minister with limited powers. The council served as the executive branch, under the guidance of a French-appointed governor.

In 1957 another RDA conference was held in Bamako. This time, however, disputes among party members emerged. Keita and his colleagues—Léopold Senghor

The coat of arms of the Republic of Mali contains several symbolic elements. The building in the center is the mosque at Djenné – a reminder that most Malians follow the Islamic religion. A rising sun is crossed by bows and arrows, above which flies a bird of prey. Beneath these images, the French words may be translated as "One People, One Goal, One Faith."

from Senegal and Sékou Touré from Guinea—viewed the RDA's cooperation with France as an attempt to weaken nationalist movements. These leaders broke with the RDA.

Soon afterward, France again reorganized its overseas holdings, offering them independence within a newly formed French Community. Along with Senegal, French Sudan voted for self-rule within the French Community in 1958, and in 1959 the two nations combined to form the Mali Federation. Senghor became the federation's president, and Keita served as prime minister. The leaders hoped the federation would bring economic and social benefits to both countries.

Political disagreements between the former colonies caused the Mali Federation to break up in August 1960. On September 22, 1960, Keita proclaimed the founding of the Republic of Mali and became its first president. The new state withdrew from the French Community and soon after abandoned the franc zone—

an economic group that used the French franc as a common form of money. For a brief time, Mali associated itself with Guinea and Ghana, but this union dissolved in 1963.

Keita's Regime

In the 1960s, Keita and his Union Soudanaise (US) party attempted a bold program of state-funded social and economic development. The new plans intended to make Mali independent of foreign influence. Keita called for the withdrawal of French soldiers stationed in Mali and demanded the return of Malian troops serving in the French armed forces. The president also halted the testing of French nuclear weapons in the Malian Sahara. Keita's economic agenda included plans for collectivization—that is, combining many small farms to increase agricultural production.

The government formed a state-owned trading company to sell Mali's goods and to buy imports on the world market. The directors of this organization found their job difficult because France, which had better relations with its other former colonies, chose not to trade with Mali. In addition, Senegal had temporarily closed the Dakar-Niger Railway to Malian traffic as a result of the breakup of the Mali Federation.

To overcome these difficulties, Mali turned for aid to the Communist governments of the Soviet Union and the People's Republic of China. Dissatisfaction arose among pro-French businesspeople, and the availability of consumer goods declined. These events led to unrest as Keita's regime became less able to meet the needs of ordinary Malians.

In 1967 Keita announced measures to combat the country's severe economic problems. He cut the value of the nation's currency by half, and later returned the debt-ridden nation to the franc zone. The public, however, was increasingly reluctant to endure the economic hardships that Keita's programs had caused.

On August 22, 1967, Keita launched a cultural revolution to rid the US party of people who opposed his ideas. Widespread removals of party officials followed at the local, regional, and national levels. Keita hoped the political activities would draw attention away from the failure of his economic policies. To further frighten his rivals, Keita increased the power of the Popular Militia—an armed segment of the

To strengthen his country's new friendship with Communist nations, Keita made a state visit to the Soviet Union in 1962. Here, he rides through the streets of the capital city of Moscow between Soviet officials Nikita Khrushchev *(left)* and Leonid Brezhnev *(right)*.

Moussa Traoré overthrew Keita's regime in 1968 and became Mali's president in 1969. Since then, the chief executive has struggled to deal with droughts and military unrest.

Union Soudanaise. The president also dissolved the national assembly.

In time, the Popular Militia became a harsh force throughout the country. Keita and his government lost support as arrests and torture created strong grass-roots opposition. The Popular Militia's increasing size and its harassment of the national army motivated some officers to act. On November 19, 1968, they overthrew the increasingly pro-Communist Keita regime. Keita was imprisoned, and the Military Committee of National Liberation (CMLN) established a temporary government.

Mali Under Traoré

The CMLN installed a new administration under a senior officer, Captain Yoro Diakité, who had served in the French army. But a junior officer, Moussa Traoré, led the actual coup d'état (government takeover). His leadership of the November overthrow established him as chief of state and president of the CMLN. In 1969 Traoré became president of Mali.

On September 22, 1976, President Traoré founded the Democratic Union of the Malian People (UDPM). The new party—the only legal political organization in Mali—was part of Traoré's plan to return the country to civilian rule.

Severe droughts that resulted in poverty and famine plagued the nation and the Traoré regime in the 1970s. Nevertheless, the president survived attempts of various army factions to overthrow his government. In 1978 opponents of civilian rule tried to dislodge Traoré, and some junior officers attempted a coup in 1980. But no independent leader or opposition political party has arisen to voice the concerns of the majority of Malians. A gap continues to exist between the few bureaucrats and urban dwellers who live rather well and the many urban and rural poor.

Throughout the 1980s, Traoré ruled a divided military committee, while moving slowly toward more civilian participation in the government. In elections held in 1985, a majority of voters reelected Traoré to the presidency for a second six-year term. Legislative elections in June 1988 gave the UDPM every seat in the national assembly. In a cabinet reshuffle the president eliminated the post of prime minister.

Yet economic, not political, issues dominate Mali's future. Relief from constant financial problems occurred in the late 1980s, when some of Mali's European creditors agreed to cancel or reschedule the nation's foreign debts. In addition, the Malian government took internal steps to improve its economic situation. The Traoré regime reorganized public finances and abandoned price restrictions on some farm products. The agricultural controls had stopped many Malian farmers from planting surplus food because they could not get a good price for their crops.

Mali also joined regional banking institutions, including the West African Monetary Union and the Central Bank of West Africa. Despite these steps, poor financial management and droughts continue to slow the nation's development.

Government

Since independence, single political parties have dominated Mali's government. The country operates as a one-party state under a mixed military-civilian regime.

The present government of Mali is based on the Constitution of 1974. The president, who serves as head of state and minister of defense, consults with a cabinet, which is composed largely of civilians. Army officers, however, control the key ministries of agriculture and planning. The number of ministers in the cabinet and their areas of responsibility frequently change.

The Malian national assembly has 82 members, who are elected to three-year terms. The legislators come from a list of candidates selected by local committees of the UDPM. The assembly meets infrequently and rarely, if ever, rejects legislation suggested by the president. The UDPM, on the other hand, may approve or disapprove the president's proposals.

Mali's judicial system, which is an arm of the executive branch, is based on the legal code used in France. Although some new legislation reflects traditional Malian ways, French colonial styles of justice still prevail in most cases. A supreme court is the highest court in the Malian justice system. Courts of appeal and lower courts exist at the local level.

For administrative purposes, Mali is divided into eight regions and the district of Bamako. These units, under the direction of appointed governors, are subgrouped into districts, *cercles* (circles), and *arrondissements* (secondary districts).

Photo by Piotr Kostrzewski

Since the Traoré government abandoned some restrictions on food prices, a wider variety of fruits, vegetables, and grains have appeared in weekly markets.

Thousands of faithful Muslims arrive in Mopti to attend an annual Islamic festival.

Photo by The Hutchison Library

3) The People

With 8.9 million inhabitants, Mali has an average of 18 people living in each square mile of its territory. This figure is one of the lowest population densities in West Africa. Yet the Malian population is distributed very unevenly, with the highest concentrations in settlements along the Niger River and throughout the central part of the nation. Another two million Malians live and work outside the country in nearby West African states, particularly Côte d'Ivoire.

Like most other African countries, Mali has a small urban population. Roughly 20 percent of the people dwell in cities. In ad-dition, most Malians are very young—about 60 percent are under the age of 20. The nation's high birthrate and short life expectancy help to explain the large percentage of youthful Malians.

Ethnic and Language Groups

As an age-old crossroads of trade, Mali contains a variety of African peoples and languages. Several large ethnic groups and a number of smaller communities exist in the country. Many of these societies share common cultural and language ties, while others are quite distinct.

In Bamako, a young Bambara woman carries her sleeping child in a sling on her back. The Bambara are Mali's largest ethnic group.

Courtesy of United Nations

The nation's largest ethnic group is the Bambara, who generally farm the land to make a living. With almost three million people, this group makes up about one-third of the population. Living mostly in the middle Niger River Valley, the Bambara speak a Mande tongue that is understood both in the capital and throughout the country.

Closely related to the Bambara are the Malinke of southwestern and western Mali. This group's main tongue is also part of the Mande language family. As heirs of the ancient Mali Empire, the 450,000 Malinke are proud of their history and traditions. Many Malinke are farmers or the recent descendants of farmers, and the group has supplied most of Mali's politicians since independence. Modibo Keita was a Malinke, as are President Traoré and numerous senior army officers.

The Fulbé and the Tukulors live in the inland delta of the Niger River and speak Fulani, which belongs to the Pular family

Women of a nomadic Fulbé family sit on mats in front of their dwelling in the Sahel. Most Fulbé are herders who travel between the inland delta and the Sahel. Some cross the border into Senegal, which also has a large Fulbé population.

Courtesy of J. Van Acker/FAO

of languages. The groups' cattle-keeping ancestors originally moved to Mali from homelands in the Senegal River Valley. Although both groups together make up less than 20 percent of the population, they claim superiority over other peoples because of their livestock-based wealth. The Fulbé and the Tukulors also take pride in the role that their communities have played in Mali's history.

This trait is also true of the 400,000 Songhai, who live in eastern Mali, and of the nation's 500,000 Soninke. The Soninke, whose ancestors were part of the Ghana Empire, make their homes in the northwestern Sahel.

The Fulbé are among the few Malians who have ready access to dairy products. Here, members of the group gather at a milk collection point.

Independent Picture Service

39

Photo by The Hutchison Library

Carrying a digging tool over his shoulder, a Dogon hunter checks the barrel of his gun. Most Dogon live in cliffside dwellings in southern and eastern Mali.

The Tuareg, who are mainly nomadic herders, are the descendants of North African Berbers. The group has long opposed the authority of the Malian government and directs its loyalty to the head of its clan. Speaking an ancient Berber tongue and using their own form of writing, the Tuareg maintain a separate lifestyle in the Malian Sahara.

Among the smaller ethnic groups in the country are the Gur-speaking Dogon, whose art forms and culture have gained worldwide fame in the past 20 years. Many young Dogon are leaving Mali for jobs in other nations. As a result, the group numbers less than 300,000. Additional members of Mali's African mixture include other peoples that speak the Gur language, such as the Senufo and the Bobo.

Photo by C. Nairn/The Hutchison Library

This Tuareg nomad wears a distinctive face covering around his head, mouth, and nose. The cloth protects him from blowing sand and grit in the Sahara. Children of the Tuareg *(right)* remain at a base camp with their mothers and help to grow vegetables and grains in small fields.

Photo by Piotr Kostrzewski

40

Few non-Africans permanently live in Mali. A small French community resides in the country as a result of commercial, educational, and administrative ties that began in colonial times. The Europeans, as well as Malian government workers, speak French—the nation's official language. A limited number of Arabs, mainly dwelling in Bamako and in a few large towns, are involved in trade.

Daily Life

Most Malians make their homes in small villages in the central savanna area and depend on the land for a living. Malian farmers produce little more than they need to feed their own families—a type of agriculture called subsistence farming.

Each village is made up of a cluster of round, straw-roofed houses constructed of sun-baked mud bricks. The dwellings are further grouped into family compounds, which usually shelter grandparents, aunts, and uncles, as well as parents, brothers, and sisters. Since Islamic laws allow Malian men to have more than one wife, families can become quite large. Indeed, some villages are made up of a single, extended family. The head of the oldest or sometimes the largest family decides which part of the village land is to be cultivated by each family group.

Malian women play a major role in farming by helping to sow and harvest crops. They also have other responsibilities, such as gathering firewood, cooking, providing water, and doing the family's laundry.

Most Malians choose to live near a good source of water, such as the Niger River. A weekly market draws villagers to the largest nearby town, where produce, fish, and other items can be bought or traded.

Photo by John Hatt/The Hutchison Library

Courtesy of Red Sea Mission Team, Inc.

In some areas, finding a water supply is difficult. Deep wells tap the reserves that lie underground, and women and children bring up the water in buckets.

These Malian mothers wait outside a rural health clinic to have their babies examined. Few such centers exist in Mali, and the nation's infant mortality rate is the highest in Africa.

Malian women carry their babies on their backs while they work and often walk with a load of wood or a container of water balanced on their heads.

The ways of ordinary Malians are in sharp constrast to the lifestyles of the nation's relatively small wealthy class or elite. These French-speaking citizens live in Bamako and in the larger regional towns. Most of them are members of the civil service or engage in commercial activities. In general, the elite carefully guards its political power to ensure that the nation's imbalanced distribution of wealth and power remains unchanged.

Health

The Malian government spends very little money to develop or improve health care and the national diet. As a result, Mali has some of the worst health statistics in the world. Thirteen percent of all Malian newborns have a lower-than-normal birth weight. About 175 Malian babies out of 1,000 die before they reach the age of one, and a large percentage of children do not live to the age of five. The average life expectancy in Mali is about 43 years.

The homes of most Malians lack sanitary facilities, and a substantial number of people are poorly nourished. Few

43

Malians receive adequate medical care, and the high death rate—especially among infants—has kept the population from growing fast.

Lack of trained medical personnel, particularly in rural areas, contributes to the poor health of most Malians. About 300 doctors and 2,000 nurses serve the entire country, and most of these professionals live in the cities. Drought and famine have further complicated the health situation, when safe water and adequate food supplies dwindle.

Education

Mali has a long heritage of educational achievement. Islamic schools date back to the thirteenth century, when teachers at Gao, Tombouctou, and Djenné attracted Muslim students throughout North Africa.

As early as 1887, the French colonial government established schools for the sons of Malian leaders. At these institutions, pupils learned the French language and absorbed French culture. Graduates helped to fill the colonial administration's labor needs.

A village elder in a northwestern settlement reads to children from a Christian book. Not many of Mali's adults can read and write, but more young people are attending school than in previous decades.

Resting their feet in fine-grained Saharan sand, these young Tuareg are learning verses from the Koran (Islam's sacred book) in a village school. Religious education has been a major force in Mali for centuries.

Since independence, Mali has attempted to improve public education. In the 1960s, the government spent more than 20 percent of its budget on education, and the number of classrooms and students increased rapidly. In the late 1980s, about 330,000 students attended primary school, and almost 40,000 received some secondary education. About 3,000 pupils are enrolled in technical and professional schools. Despite these figures, however, the majority of adult Malians cannot read and write, and only 10 percent of the entire population is literate.

Although the state funds most educational programs, Roman Catholic religious orders run a number of elementary and adult teaching centers. Since Mali does not have any universities or colleges, more than 1,500 Malians study overseas in France, Canada, the United States, and Eastern Europe. University instruction is available only to the small percentage of the population that has enough money and political influence to gain access to further schooling.

Religion

The Islamic religion unites most Malians, 90 percent of whom support the faith. Established in Saudi Arabia in the seventh century A.D., Islam spread through the Middle East to many parts of Africa and Asia. Muhammad, the religion's founder, described the principles of Islam as revealed to him by Allah (the Arabic word for God). These ideas have been collected in the Koran, the book of Islamic sacred writings.

Faithful Muslims perform certain duties, including praying daily, donating to the poor, and fasting during the holy month of Ramadan. In addition, male Muslims are encouraged to make a pilgrimage to Mecca—Islam's holy city in Saudi Arabia—

45

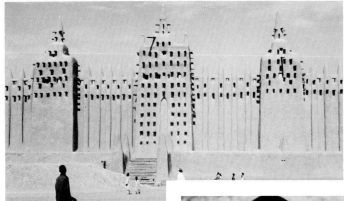

The mosque at Djenné has inspired building styles for holy places in Mopti *(pictured)* and other cities.

Five times each day, faithful Muslims pray to Allah (Islam's word for God). Believers turn toward the city of Mecca in Saudi Arabia, where the Islamic religion originated. About 90 percent of Mali's population follows Islam.

The Dogon, who continue to support centuries-old African beliefs, include masked dances in their rituals.

once in their lifetime. Most Malians, however, cannot afford this journey.

Some Malian Muslims also follow Islamic *tariqas*—powerful religious brotherhoods. These organizations, such as the Tijaniya and the Qadiriya brotherhoods, wield political influence because they often control how their followers vote. The Hamallist tariqa is an Islamic splinter group prominent in the towns of Nioro du Sahel and Yélimané in western Mali. A few wealthy merchants, especially in Bamako, belong to the conservative Wahabiya brotherhood.

About 9 percent of Malians continue to honor traditional African beliefs that focus on a universal life force in nature. These believers seek to control this vital power for practical ends, such as to secure a good job or to reap a big harvest. As a result of French influence, a small percentage of Malians follow Christianity, principally Roman Catholicism.

The Arts

Malian craftspeople focus their creative energies on making wood, metal, leather, and woven goods. They produce excellent pottery, woven mats, wooden masks, iron tools, and handmade textiles. Western-influenced artists create watercolor and oil paintings, and self-trained artisans fashion wall paintings that depict scenes from daily life.

Another major art form that flourishes in Mali is popular music. Talented players establish dance bands in Bamako and some of the regional towns. These groups use modern electronic equipment and play popular tunes drawn from all over the world. The best groups produce original Malian music that reflects the tradition of the *griot*. Ancient griots were royal storytellers, but present-day griots mix tales and music for the enjoyment of ordinary people. A griot often strums a *kora*, a 21-stringed instrument, and may be accompanied by a musician playing a *balaphon* (a wooden xylophone). One of Mali's leading kora players is the young Malinke Toumani Diabete, who blends his music with that of other countries.

Performances of the National Folklore Troupe of Mali include authentic dances

Toumani Diabete, a young Malinke *kora* player, uses his instrument to produce an unusual blend of traditional and modern sounds. The kora consists of a leather-covered half-gourd through which a long wooden pole passes. When struck, the instrument's 21 strings give a broad range of tones.

Photo by Jak Kilby

Courtesy of United Nations

The Malian historian and diplomat Amadou Hampate Ba *(wearing glasses)* has preserved many of the nation's folk stories. For several years after independence, Ba also served as Mali's ambassador to Côte d'Ivoire. In 1967, however, when political events in Mali became chaotic, he was removed from office. Remaining in Côte d'Ivoire, Ba returned to his homeland only after President Modibo Keita's regime had been overthrown.

47

Modern rock paintings *(above),* **traditional pottery** *(bottom left),* **and wood carvings** *(bottom right)* **are all part of Mali's age-old artistic output.**

Courtesy of Tom O'Toole

At streetside, a woman sells cups of milk to passersby. Few Malians regularly eat dairy products or meat, both of which are not readily available.

and music of the Bambara, Senufo, and Malinke peoples. The troupe has added materials from the Fulbé, Tuareg, and Dogon to create a national collection. Throughout Mali, musical styles that incorporate elements of traditional religious beliefs continue to be performed in villages.

Malian scholars, such as Bokar N'Diaye and Amadou Hampate Ba, have published a number of poems and have brought together many traditional Malian oral legends and folk stories. Djibril Tamsir Niane has written the story of Sundiata, the founder of the Mali Empire, in the Malinke language. A few young Malinke writers have begun to compose ethnic verse, and in the countryside people still recite ancient poems and ballads.

Food

Three crops—millet (a cereal grain), cassava (a root crop), and maize (corn)—provide the basic food for most Malians.

Courtesy of Lester and Rosemary Moeller

A display of red peppers attracts a customer to a market stall in Mopti.

After being ground by hand with a long wooden pole, millet is made into porridge. Malians eat cassava raw, or bake it in the embers of small fires, or soak and grate it into flour. Cassava flour has almost no nutritional value, although it can be stored for weeks and is easy to transport. Many Malian farmers also grow corn, which is often eaten on the cob.

Most Malians survive on a simple diet of rice, millet, cassava, sorghum (a grain), and maize. Few Malians can afford to eat meat every day, and many do not have it even once a week. In regions that lie near rivers and streams, however, dried, fresh, or smoked fish sometimes is served at mealtimes. Wealthy urban dwellers, in contrast, often dine on chicken, goat, beef, fruit, and vegetables.

A meal in an urban restaurant or among the rich might consist of grilled beef, a salad of lettuce, tomatoes, and onions, and deep-fried strips of cassava. Dessert could include fresh melons, papayas (large, oblong, yellow fruit), or mangoes. Traditionally, three glasses of very sweet green tea follow the meal. Other specialties are peanut-flavored chicken stew over rice and freshly caught Nile perch—called *capitaine* in Mali—served with a spicy sauce.

Photo by Chris Johnson/The Hutchison Library

Throughout many parts of the country, women pound grain into a coarse flour with long wooden poles. The flour is then made into porridge—a staple of the Malian diet.

In a large plaza in front of Djenné's Grand Mosque, covered and open booths offer food, textiles, baskets, and other items to eager customers. Most Malians earn little money, and marketplaces offer opportunities to trade as well as to buy.

4) The Economy

Mali is among the world's 10 poorest nations. Its average income per person is less than $200 annually. The country has few mineral deposits, and most of the soil is not very fertile. Only in southern Mali is rainfall sufficient to grow crops without irrigation. In addition, the nation lacks its own seaport and has few good roads. The inferior condition of the railway link through Senegal also hampers economic development.

The most serious obstacle to progress, however, has been the badly managed, state-dominated economic system. Small, government-financed programs continue to depend on France, West Germany, the Soviet Union, and other non-African countries for funds. Many industries close or lose money because of poor management and corruption.

In recent years, the Traoré government has begun to reassess its financial plans. The nation's unsuccessful economic programs have been reorganized, and this move has attracted more foreign aid. The administration has also renewed its efforts to establish cooperation among West African states on issues of mutual benefit.

Agriculture

Although less than 10 percent of the country's land is suitable for crops, the Malian economy is based on agriculture and on raising livestock. Farming employs at least 90 percent of the country's population. After they feed their families, most farmers do not have any food left to sell at markets. Cotton and livestock are the major export earners, accounting for more than 90 percent of the nation's foreign income.

Droughts in the 1970s and 1980s have decreased yields of both cash (money-earning) crops and other food items. An inadequate transportation network limits the ability of individuals to get their crops and animals to a central market. In addition, low, state-controlled prices for agricultural goods have discouraged farmers from producing surplus food because earnings fall short of cultivation costs.

TRADITIONAL FARMING

Most Malians cultivate the land by using a slash-and-burn technique. Farm workers clear away vegetation by cutting it down. The stubble of the plants is then burned—a process that also makes the soil fertile for a few years. After the plot has been planted with food crops, farmers use simple tools, such as short-handled hoes and animal-drawn plows, to tend the field. Rice and sugarcane are grown in central Mali, and millet, corn, and vegetables thrive in the south.

Courtesy of J. Van Acker/FAO

Using an ox-drawn plow, two farm workers turn over the dry soil of a field near Niono in central Mali.

This woman wields a traditional hand tool to till her plot. Areas in southern Mali receive enough rainfall to grow a variety of crops.

Non-cultivated items, such as shea nuts, are almost as important as cultivated products in providing food to the population. The best land is reserved for cash crops. Less-fertile plots are set aside for cassava and sorghum, which thrive in poor soil and need little care. As a result, many Malians are undernourished because the health-giving foods are sold, while poor crops form the basic Malian diet.

CASH CROPS AND LIVESTOCK

In the 1920s and 1930s, the French introduced two major cash crops—peanuts and cotton. Since then, acreages reserved for these crops have steadily increased,

A nomadic Tuareg herder brings his livestock to a watering point in the Sahel. Droughts in the 1980s have hampered the ability of some Malians to raise goats and cattle.

53

A threshing machine cuts stalks of grain on a government-owned farm in Baguineda, southern Mali.

When rainfall levels are normal, cattle – one of Mali's main livestock species – find plenty of seasonal grazing land in the Sahel.

Since modern machinery is scarce in Mali, large farms still rely on oxen as labor animals. Huge fields continue to be planted and harvested using simple manual methods.

although market prices have varied. With extensive irrigation, cotton can be planted in the south, and peanuts grow well in the west.

Cattle are raised throughout Mali, mostly by nomadic herding peoples, such as the Tuareg. Many of the animals belonging to the Tuareg died during the droughts of the 1970s and 1980s, but herds have nearly reached pre-drought levels once again. Selective breeding and pasture improvements have not yet been tried widely. As a result, many animals suffer from disease and do not have enough grazing land. Goats and sheep roam freely in most areas of the country, as do chickens, guinea fowls, turkeys, ducks, horses, and donkeys.

The bulk of the nation's saleable livestock is the property of a few wealthy people. Through a series of state-controlled companies, the government has sought to establish modern livestock-raising projects in central Mali. But small-scale operations continue to dominate the livestock sector. Traditional herders are reluctant to part with their animals because the herds are signs of wealth and importance.

As his son watches, a man skillfully butchers a goat, removing its hide and skin and exposing its inner organs.

55

Fishing

Mali's fishing industry is concentrated in the Niger and Bani rivers, in their tributaries, and in a few lakes, particularly Lake Debo. The Niger alone contains over 180 species of fish, including carp, catfish, and perch. These marine animals follow the flood pattern of the rivers and streams, and fishermen live a semi-nomadic lifestyle in search of their daily catch. They pull about 100,000 tons of fish from Malian waters every year. The Traoré government intends to expand the fishing industry, which already employs about 200,000 people, by building small factories to store and package the fish.

The center of Mali's fishing industry is Mopti, where workers process and market much of the nation's freshwater catch. Villagers along the banks of the rivers prepare the fish for sale by smoking, drying, and salting them. These processed food products contribute significantly to Mali's foreign income. Most of the fish go to other countries in West Africa, particularly Burkina Faso and Côte d'Ivoire.

Photo by Piotr Kostrzewski

Men of the Bozo people—one of Mali's many small ethnic groups—are mainly seasonal fishermen on the Niger River. Moving up and down the river, the Bozo propel their vessels with poles to new fishing grounds and store their daily catch in the bottom of their boats.

Courtesy of United Nations

A worker carries a basketful of dried fish from Mopti's wharf to the city's market. Improvements in storing, processing, and packing have decreased the number of fish lost through spoiling. Better roads out of Mopti, which lies along the inland delta, have also boosted exports.

57

This young Saharan is among the traders who bring the annual shipment of salt from mines at Taoudenni to the market at Tombouctou.

Mining and Manufacturing

In western Mali, particularly near Kayes, are considerable quantities of iron ore and bauxite (the raw material from which aluminum is obtained). A relatively large deposit of phosphate lies in the Gao region and has encouraged a mining venture that produces about 2,000 tons of much-needed fertilizer every year. Mali also contains manganese and lithium reserves near Kayes and Bougouni. Workers have chipped away at a marble deposit at Bafoulabé for local needs, and a large limestone quarry furnishes raw material for a Soviet-built cement factory.

Salt deposits at Taoudenni in northern Mali have been mined for at least a thousand years. About 3,000 tons of salt are shipped annually from this remote area. The gold stock of the southwest, which miners have extracted for centuries, is once again providing income. West German and Japanese firms have signed contracts to obtain radioactive source materials, such

Long strands of thread are connected to the handlooms of weavers in a Malian village. Much of the nation's cloth is produced in this traditional way.

as uranium, in Mali. The materials are needed to produce nuclear energy.

Until recently, state-funded companies controlled most of Mali's small industrial output. These firms included textile factories, a cement plant in Kayes, a peanut oil and soap complex in Koulikoro, and a canning factory in Baguineda. A sugar refinery operates south of Bamako, and rice-processing plants lie in the inland delta. The capital also has a number of industrial sites that produce ceramics, matches, cigarettes, leather, beer, and furniture.

A textile mill in Ségou processes some of the country's cotton crop into thread.

Courtesy of Janise Baker

Photo by The Hutchison Library

Not much hard stone exists in Mali, and most buildings use mud bricks as the basic structural material.

Courtesy of Deborah Dyson

A small barge on the Niger carries a car from one side of the river to the other. Waterways play a major role in landlocked Mali's transportation network.

Transportation and Energy

Mali, like other West African countries, has changed its basic form of transport from small river craft and human porters to trains, aircraft, barges, and motor vehicles. In the late 1980s, Mali had 1,000 miles of paved roads, and a major highway connected Bamako to Mopti. This route has opened the Dogon country to tourism and has made it easier to ship fish taken from the Niger and Bani rivers to export markets.

Another road goes south, providing access to ports in Côte d'Ivoire. An 84-mile highway connects Mali with Ouagadougou, the capital of Burkina Faso, and with the railroad that runs to Abidjan, Côte d'Ivoire. Other linkages include a 357-mile road between Sévaré and Gao and a

345-mile route from Gao to the Algerian border. These thoroughfares will eventually be part of the paved Trans-Saharan Highway linking Algeria with Nigeria. Mali also has about 6,000 miles of unpaved roads, which are passable most of the year.

The French laid the first railway lines in Mali in the 1880s. France's aim was to connect its Atlantic ports with inland areas and the Mediterranean shore. More than a century later, the track stretches for 800 miles, but constant maintenance is required to keep trains running. The railway is still inadequate for the volume of traffic that uses it.

Transportation on the Niger River has improved in recent years. The waterway is navigable from Guinea to Niger between late August and January, depending on

Courtesy of Red Sea Mission Team, Inc.

Camels are still a reliable form of travel in both the Sahel and the Sahara.

Few roads exist in Mali, and most of the routes are not paved. When rains are heavy, paths like this one to Djenné nearly disappear.

Sikasso lacks good inner-city connections, so this resident brings his produce to market by bicycle.

The capital city of Bamako is one of the few places where buses, taxis, and other motorized vehicles are readily available.

Boats commonly ferry goods and people to many parts of Mali. When the vessels are weighed down by being overcrowded, however, they can become stuck in shallow water.

For most Malians, wood is still the main source of everyday fuel. Here, women bargain at the wood market in Ségou.

the rains. Boats can travel on the Senegal River from Kayes to Saint-Louis in Senegal between late July and October. This connection gives Mali part-time access to an Atlantic seaport—a major consideration for a landlocked, trade-dependent nation.

Air Mali, which was a state-owned enterprise until 1985, handles domestic airline traffic on an irregular basis. An international airport opened outside Bamako in late 1975 to accommodate planes from other parts of West Africa and from Europe. In general, however, most Malians rely on walking to get around and often travel long distances on foot.

Hydroelectric power plants supply about half of Mali's electricity needs. These installations harness the power of rivers that flow in the southern part of the country. Petroleum fills much of the remainder of the nation's fuel requirements. Lacking its own oil resources, Mali imports petroleum and petroleum-based products from Côte d'Ivoire.

The Future

A poor nation largely dependent on farming, Mali faces difficult challenges. Unpredictable harvests, unwise farm policies, and long dry spells have seriously affected the economy. In addition, inadequate food and water supplies have caused the health of Malians to decline and have disrupted traditional patterns of living.

Although the government has attempted to address some of these needs, much remains to be done to improve the Malian standard of living. One hopeful sign is the amount of foreign aid that Mali has been able to attract. These funds will allow the nation to focus on immediate internal problems. If the government continues to reorganize public finances and to renew the agricultural sector, Malians may yet escape the cycle of poverty and drought that has dominated their lives in recent decades.

Photo by The Hutchison Library

Using well-worn paths, ordinary citizens in Mali still go from place to place on foot.

Photo by Piotr Kostrzewski

The lives of these Malinke women and children may improve as a result of new government efforts to reorganize the Malian economy.

63

Index